D0004712

What Were the Roaring Twenties?

by Michele Mortlock

illustrated by Jake Murray

Penguin Workshop
An Imprint of Penguin Random House

For my grandmother, Mary Wiseman Welling,
who survived the Spanish flu—MM

For my wife, Krysti. You're the bee's knees!—JM

PENGUIN WORKSHOP
Penguin Young Readers Group
An Imprint of Penguin Random House LLC

Library of Congress Cataloging-in-Publication Data is available.

ISBN 9781524786380 (paperback)   10 9 8 7 6 5 4 3 2 1
ISBN 9781524786397 (library binding)   10 9 8 7 6 5 4 3 2 1

Contents

What Were the Roaring Twenties?

Not every period in United States history is special enough to have a nickname. But the 1920s has more than one. These years are called the Roaring Twenties, the Jazz Age, and even the New Era. Why? What made this time so special? What made the twenties roar?

It's because these years were exciting . . . fun . . . dangerous . . . and even silly. There were crazy fads such as flagpole sitting, which started in 1924 when stuntman Alvin "Shipwreck" Kelly took a dare from a friend. He sat on top of a flagpole for thirteen hours and thirteen minutes. Soon Kelly was hired all across the United States to repeat the stunt. Other daredevils imitated him, competing for money. Records were set for twelve days, seventeen days, and even twenty-one days, with food sent up in baskets. Huge crowds gathered to watch.

There were also dance marathons, often called "bunion derbies" or "corn and callus carnivals." For twenty-five cents, spectators watched couples dance for hours, days, or sometimes even weeks. After a while, all that contestants could do was shuffle their feet or cling to the necks of their partners and be dragged along. All to earn the first-place prize money.

The twenties also were known for thrilling feats of a more important nature. In 1927, pilot Charles Lindbergh became the first to fly nonstop

across the Atlantic Ocean—and he did it all alone in a small plane that didn't even have a parachute.

Most of all, the 1920s were famous for good times—listening to jazz bands in nightclubs, dancing the Charleston, dashing around in newly affordable automobiles, and following the lives of glamorous Hollywood movie stars. However, the good times didn't last. On October 29, 1929, it all came crashing down, in an abrupt and terrible end.

CHAPTER 1
After the Great War

The 1920s certainly didn't start out being a whole lot of fun. In the beginning of the decade, the United States was recovering from two terrible disasters.

The first was World War I, which ended in 1918 with over seventeen million people dead, both soldiers and civilians. The United States

joined the war near the end, but in only nineteen months, more than one hundred thousand US soldiers were killed fighting overseas and another two hundred thousand were wounded.

Then a different, totally unexpected enemy appeared: the Spanish flu. This deadly strain of the flu virus spread quickly around the world. It killed 675,000 people in the United States, far more than the war had.

The flu killed very quickly, within hours or days. Most of its victims were young, healthy adults. New Yorker Lillian Goldsmith often recalled that her sister Vivian "was dancing at a party on Friday and dead on Monday." At first, the symptoms seemed like any other flu, with fever and headaches. Sometimes patients recovered. But if they didn't, their lungs and internal organs were destroyed, and their bodies would turn blue.

There was no cure.

After so much tragedy, many people—especially the young and the returning soldiers—were desperate to have a good time. They blamed the horrible war on the older generation. Now was the time to leave the past behind.

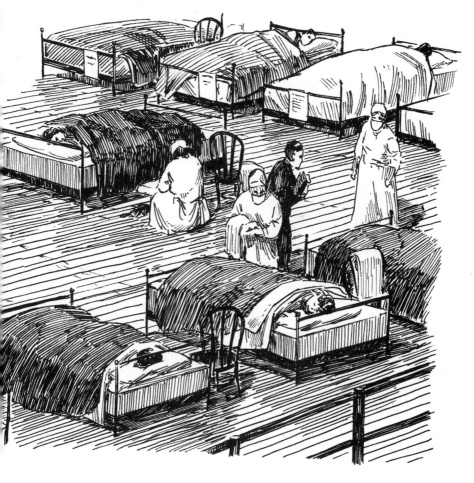

Return to Normalcy

After the war, millions of Americans wanted the country to go back to the way it was before. In 1920, Ohio senator Warren G. Harding ran for president.

His campaign slogan was "Return to Normalcy." Harding won but gave important positions to unqualified people and paid little attention to what they did. His administration was rocked by scandals.

Warren G. Harding

He died suddenly in 1923, before his term was over, and Vice President Calvin Coolidge became president.

It took a little while for the twenties to really roar. After the war, the US economy went into a slump. Factories that once had been working overtime to provide weapons and supplies for American troops closed. Companies went out of business. People lost their jobs. Returning soldiers looking for work added to the numbers of unemployed.

The government, however, found ways to help. And by 1921, the economy turned around. There were more jobs, which put more money in the pockets of the American public. A spending boom began. The New Era had arrived.

CHAPTER 2
Women Voters

On August 18, 1920, there was a dramatic change in the lives of American women: They were finally granted the right to vote. It was a right they had spent over seventy years fighting to win. With the vote, women had the power to change laws and to take a greater part in government. This led to a greater desire to take control of their lives. Women stepped out of the shadows of their parents and husbands. They went out by themselves, without any chaperones to supervise them on dates. More girls went to college. In 1918, only 13,491 women earned a college degree. In 1930, the number had climbed to 55,266.

Before the war, jobs for women had been

limited. The poor had to settle for low-paying jobs, such as doing housework in other people's homes. For middle-class women, nursing and teaching were among the few careers open to them. Being a doctor, lawyer, or head of a company was practically unheard of.

During the war, however, women had taken the jobs of men fighting overseas. They were streetcar operators. They worked in shipyards, steel mills, and factories that made guns and ammunition. Although many of those jobs were lost when the men came back, more and more women kept on collecting paychecks. They found other careers. Growing businesses now needed secretaries, stenographers, typists, and file clerks in their offices. These jobs were usually filled by women.

While most women still stayed at home to take care of their families, their lives changed a lot, too, during the 1920s. New inventions made it possible to spend less time doing chores and to have more time for fun.

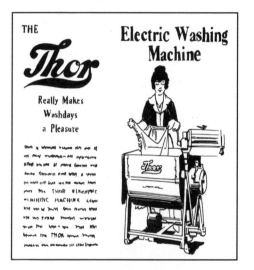

Electricity had been lighting up city streets since the late 1800s. Now more private homes became wired for electricity. Housekeeping became much easier with electric appliances like washing machines, stoves, refrigerators, vacuum cleaners, and sewing machines.

Ironing Out a Problem

Before electricity, an iron either had to be placed in a fire to get hot or it was heated by fuels such as kerosene, which could catch fire. Constant care was needed over the temperature of the iron. If it wasn't hot enough, it wouldn't press out wrinkles. If it was too hot, it would burn the fabric. One way to test the iron was to spit on the hot metal. If it sizzled, it was time to start ironing! New electric irons made pressing clothes so much easier, faster, and far less dangerous.

In 1924, Clarence Birdseye invented frozen foods. Meals became easier to prepare—they didn't have to be made from scratch. Convenient products like Wonder Bread, Welch's Grape Jelly, Kool-Aid, and Rice Krispies came on the market.

There was a huge revolution in women's fashions. Before, women wore stiff, heavy clothing—dresses with high collars, big sleeves, tight corsets, and bulky, floor-length skirts. Now women wanted loose, comfortable clothes so they could do the new fast dances like the bunny hop, the Charleston, and the Lindy. They wanted to play sports. They didn't want to spend a lot of time getting dressed. Young women began

A woman in the early 1900s   A 1920s flapper

wearing short dresses made of lightweight fabrics that hung loose on their bodies. These new styles were much easier to wear. Mannish styles like tailored suits became popular. Some women even wore pants! A lot of older people were absolutely scandalized!

Men's Hair and Clothes

Men's clothes changed, too. Trousers became wider, with a sharp crease down the center. For casual wear, white trousers and V-neck sweaters, like those worn by tennis players, became popular. Football star Red Grange made the raccoon coat a fashion statement for men. As for their hair, men

wore it slicked back, sometimes using a cream like Brilliantine so it looked as shiny as patent leather.

Women changed their hair as well as their clothes. In the past, proper ladies had kept their long hair pinned on top of their heads. Now girls all over the country were inspired by movie stars like Clara Bow. They cut their hair in a short, sleek style called a bob. A bob was easier to care for and felt freer, which was perfect for the new, independent American woman. Opera singer Mary Garden said in an interview, "Bobbed hair belongs to the age of freedom, frankness, and progressiveness." Since there weren't a lot of hair salons, young ladies stood in long lines outside of men's barbershops to get their hair cut.

Hats and Headbands

Certain accessories came into style with the bob. The bobby pin got its name from holding the new cut in place. Snug-fitting hats, like the cloche, became fashionable. At night, headbands decorated with feathers or elaborate jewels dressed up the simple hairstyle.

These modern young women became known as flappers. No one knows for sure where the name came from, but everyone in the '20s knew what it meant. Flappers wore makeup, drove cars, and went to lots of parties. They drank cocktails and smoked cigarettes. Everything they did was considered unladylike. But they didn't care about breaking old rules—or new ones. They flocked to speakeasies and nightclubs, where they could buy drinks, even though Prohibition had made it against the law, something you could be arrested for.

CHAPTER 3
Prohibition

In 1920, the Eighteenth Amendment to the Constitution had a major impact on Americans. This amendment prohibited— made it illegal—to sell or make any kind of alcohol for drinking. This included beer and wine, as well as all kinds of liquor.

By the later part of the 1800s, two groups had formed: the American Temperance Society and the Women's Christian Temperance Union. They believed that drinking liquor was evil and that men who went to bars (where women weren't allowed) drank too much.

A drinking problem often meant men couldn't hold jobs, couldn't take care of their wives and children, and might even abandon their families.

Temperance members would march to saloons and demand that they be closed down. Some people would go even further, entering with axes and destroying every barrel and bottle that they could find. Over the years, these temperance groups became very powerful politically. And finally their cause became the law.

Although plenty of citizens obeyed the new law, many ignored it.

People who wanted to drink alcohol found many ways to do so. The new amendment actually said nothing about drinking alcohol or privately owning it. So some people bought and stored as much as they could while it was still legal to buy. Others made it themselves. Bootleggers were people who built machines for making liquor or created bathtub gin.

There wasn't enough homemade liquor to meet the demand. Since other countries didn't have Prohibition, liquor would be smuggled down from Canada. It arrived in trucks or in airplanes, or was shipped in on boats that managed to slip

past the Coast Guard. A line of ships, known as Rum Row, would wait just outside the three-mile limit in international waters. Tiny speedboats would come out at night, load the illegal cargo from the ships, and race back to shore.

Bathtub Gin

Bathtub gin was made by taking industrial alcohol, which could be very poisonous, and mixing it with a lot of water to make it safer to drink. Then things like juniper berries were added to give it flavor. Sometimes the taste was still very bad, so people would mix it with soft drinks. This kind of liquor was called "bathtub gin" because of where it was made—the bathroom tub. People had to be careful about drinking bathtub gin. Some homemade brews used dangerous ingredients like embalming fluid or mercury. People could get sick or die from drinking it.

Local smugglers and bootleggers were soon pushed aside by criminal gangs whose members were called mobsters. They built their own distilleries and breweries, and they opened bars where they could sell the illegal alcoholic drinks. Speakeasies were run in secret, behind locked doors in old buildings. You needed a password to get inside. In 1925, it was estimated that New York City alone had over thirty thousand speakeasies.

1920s Slang

Baloney: Nonsense

Bee's knees: The best

Beat it: Go away, or get lost

Cat's meow: The best

Dolled up: Dressed up

Dough: Money

Gold digger: A woman who is with a man

    for his money

Hot: Stolen

In a jam: In trouble

Java: Coffee

Pipe down: Stop talking

Real McCoy: The real thing

Swanky: Fashionable

Wet blanket: No fun at all

Nightclubs were fancier than speakeasies and were out in the open. Owners bribed government agents, police, and local politicians to leave their clubs alone, or at least give a warning before a raid. Then all the liquor could be hidden by the time the police arrived.

The illegal alcohol business was worth so much money that mobs fought with one another to gain more areas where only a certain gang could supply liquor. There were shootouts in the streets using sawed-off shotguns and Thompson submachine guns (tommy guns). Sometimes there were bombings.

Tommy gun

This gang rivalry led up to the St. Valentine's Day Massacre on February 14, 1929, in Chicago. A black car pulled up to a garage run by George "Bugs" Moran and his North Side Gang. Four men got out and entered the garage. Two were dressed as police officers. Two looked like detectives. Witnesses on the street suddenly heard a lot of gunshots inside the garage. All four men ran out, jumped into the black car, and sped away.

Inside the garage, six of Moran's men lay

dead, and one was wounded but died later. They had been lined up against a wall and shot. The phony policemen had been sent by Al "Scarface" Capone. He was the head of a rival mob and the most powerful gangster in Chicago.

Despite the crime and violence, people still went to mob-owned clubs and speakeasies. They went to these places not just to drink but also to listen to the sounds of jazz—the hottest new music in the country.

Al Capone (1899–1947)

Al "Scarface" Capone was born Alphonse Capone in Brooklyn, New York, the son of Italian immigrants.

 He dropped out of school at fourteen and started to work for the local mob, getting his nickname when he was slashed across the face in a knife fight. He moved to Chicago, where at one time he controlled ten thousand speakeasies as well as all the sale of alcohol from the Canadian border down to Florida. He was finally arrested and convicted, and he served some time in Alcatraz, the famous prison in San Francisco Bay.

CHAPTER 4
Red-Hot Jazz

Jazz was created by African American musicians in New Orleans, Louisiana. It began in the late 1890s and early 1900s. Jazz mixed together many different musical styles and traditions: West African rhythms and the folk music of African Americans, military brass bands, gospels sung in church, blues, and ragtime.

Musical Roots

Gospel music: Gospel music has its roots in the spirituals (religious songs) created by African slaves in America. Most of the singing was done without instruments, and rhythm was created by hand clapping and foot stomping. In many African American churches, gospel is still sung.

Blues: A slow, sad style of music developed from slave work songs. The songs are often about hardship, an unhappy life, or love gone wrong. Urban blues led the way to rhythm and blues and rock and roll.

Ragtime: A lively type of music that was popular from the 1890s to about 1920. It was played mostly on the piano, with the right hand playing a bouncy offbeat melody and the left hand playing a regular rhythm of base notes and chords.

Jazz depends on brass or reed instruments like saxophones, trumpets, and trombones. These instruments can slide between traditional notes, producing unusual notes that have a different pitch and are not on the same musical scale. The effect is called a bent note or blue note. Blue notes can sound happy, sad, or angry, and they give passion and feeling to the music.

Saxophone

The rhythm of jazz is different. The beat comes from all the instruments in the band, not just the drums. The rhythms can also shift or change in unexpected ways, from a strong beat to a softer beat.

Improvisation—making up music as you're playing—is also an important part of jazz. At nightclubs, the musicians didn't play a jazz number exactly as it was written. In fact, many jazz musicians couldn't read music. So they might change the rhythm, the melody, or the harmony.

This all blended into a kind of music that was full of surprise, emotion, energy, and excitement. It had a lively beat that made people want to get up and dance.

In New York City, fashionable white people traveled uptown to nightclubs like the Cotton Club, owned by mobster Owney Madden. There, they could hear great jazz musicians like Louis Armstrong and Duke Ellington.

Voices of the Jazz Age

Duke Ellington (1899–1974): Edward Kennedy "Duke" Ellington learned to play the piano at seven and took up playing jazz when he was a teenager. In 1923, he became the bandleader of a jazz orchestra. Often working with others, Ellington wrote more than one thousand compositions, made many records, performed in several films, and composed stage musicals. His career lasted his entire life.

Louis Armstrong (1901–1971): Louis Armstrong gained fame in the 1920s as a creative trumpet and cornet player. He was a major influence in

jazz, famous for his solo spots. His gravelly voice was instantly recognizable on any song, and he also appeared in several movies.

Louis Armstrong

Ethel Waters (1896–1977): Ethel Waters was one of the most popular African American singers and actresses of the 1920s. Originally touring in vaudeville shows as a singer and dancer, she made her recording debut in 1921. Later she appeared in musical revues and movies. She was a big star on Broadway in the 1930s and was nominated for a best supporting actress Academy Award in 1949 for her role in the movie *Pinky*.

Bessie Smith (1894–1937): Bessie Smith's powerful voice made her the most popular female blues singer of the 1920s and 1930s. A headlining performer, she was nicknamed "the Empress of the Blues." Her first record was in 1923, and she went on to make a total of 160.

Bessie Smith

However, even though the Cotton Club was in Harlem, there were no black customers. It was for whites only. So African Americans opened their own clubs, like the Savoy Ballroom.

Soon, jazz spread beyond the clubs. White musicians started playing it. People all over the country listened on radios or record players. Bands even toured in Europe. Jazz was the sound of modern America. That's why the 1920s also became known as the Jazz Age.

CHAPTER 5
The Harlem Renaissance

During World War I and in the 1920s, about a million African Americans left farms in the South and moved to towns and cities up north. This was the beginning of what became known as the Great Migration.

Segregation and Jim Crow Laws

In Northern cities, black people coming from the South found a somewhat better life. Although they were still barred from many opportunities open to white people, they no longer encountered the Jim Crow laws of the South. These laws restricted the lives of Southern African Americans in almost

every way. African Americans weren't allowed to go to "white" hotels or restaurants. Black children couldn't go to the same schools as white children or even use the same public water fountains. Still worse was the threat of the Ku Klux Klan (KKK), a hate group formed in the South that terrorized African Americans through beatings, kidnappings, and murder.

A KKK march in Washington, DC, in 1925

By 1920, there were between 175,000 and 200,000 African Americans living in Harlem, a neighborhood of roughly three square miles in upper Manhattan. Most had come looking for jobs, a better life, and freedom from the terrible prejudice they'd known before.

Such a large number of African Americans in one place made Harlem a city within a city. It became a community proud to celebrate its own

culture and racial identity.

Far from lower "white" Manhattan, African Americans started their own companies, ate in their own restaurants, and read their own magazines and newspapers. They went to their own movie theaters to see films made by African American filmmakers starring African American actors. They created their own libraries, schools, and even their own police force.

Madam C. J. Walker (1867–1919)

Sarah Breedlove, known as Madam C. J. Walker, was a phenomenally successful African American businesswoman. The first free-born child in her family, she was famous for creating a line of hair-care products for black women, and traveled around the country promoting them. She trained other women to become "beauty culturists" for her sales force and advertised in African American newspapers and magazines. Madam C. J. Walker became the first female self-made millionaire in the United States.

This vibrant time became known as the Harlem Renaissance. (A renaissance is a period of great creative energy.) The Harlem Renaissance produced an amazing number of gifted artists and authors.

Langston Hughes was an award-winning poet, novelist, and newspaper columnist who wrote about the lives and struggles of working-class African Americans. Zora Neale Hurston was a

Langston Hughes   Zora Neale Hurston

renowned novelist who also wrote about African American folklore after graduating from Barnard College, part of Columbia University.

Paul Robeson was an exceptional actor who won acclaim on Broadway and in the movies. He had a very deep bass voice and was a popular concert singer. He was also one of the first black men to play serious roles in the white theater, such as his starring role in Shakespeare's *Othello*.

Years later, Romare Bearden and Jacob Lawrence painted scenes of what life was like during the Harlem Renaissance. Today their works hang in important museums such as the Museum of Fine Arts in Boston and the Museum of Modern Art in New York City.

The Harlem Renaissance marked a cultural, intellectual, and artistic moment—one that had an impact well beyond the borders of Harlem. It helped bring the culture and talent of African Americans to a wider audience in the United States and around the world.

CHAPTER 6
America on the Move

Automobiles weren't new at the start of the twenties, but up until then they were expensive—way out of the reach of ordinary people. In 1900, there were only eight thousand cars in the country. That's because they were built one by one by skilled workers and took time to complete.

Henry Ford had a different idea. He would build cars quickly, make them cheaper, and sell a lot of them. His Ford Model T took only ninety-three minutes to build. By 1918, two and a half million

Henry Ford

Fords—half of all the cars on the road—had been sold. The price dropped from $850 to $360.

How did Ford do it?

By making cars on a moving assembly line.

In Ford's factory assembly line, building a car was broken down into a series of separate tasks.

Each worker stayed in one place on the moving line and had only one job to do—for example, putting on the fenders—which he did over and over again. After his job was finished, the partially built car moved down the line to the next worker who completed his task—perhaps attaching the wheels.

By the time the car reached the end of the line, it was ready for the road. By the late twenties, a Model T car rolled off the line every twenty-four seconds.

Ford also came up with a way to make it easier to pay for a car, by starting something known as the installment plan. Customers didn't have to put down all the money for a car at the time they bought it. Instead, right then they only needed to pay a small part of the cost. They would pay the rest over time in monthly installments. This meant that working Americans who didn't have a lot of money in the bank could still own a car. In 1925, three-quarters of all US cars were bought on what was called credit.

In response to all these cars, state and local governments built networks of paved, weatherproof roads across the country. By the middle of the decade, forty thousand miles were added every year. These new roads made it possible for drivers to live farther from their jobs.

Families moved from the city to the suburbs—new communities built in what had once been the countryside. Here families could live in their own house—not a cramped apartment—and children could play in a yard instead of on city streets. People with jobs in the city could drive back and forth every day.

In order to commute, more than good roads were needed. There had to be places to buy gas or get a car fixed. Service stations became a familiar sight along roads. Motorists on a long trip needed restaurants to eat at and someplace comfortable to spend the night. Motor hotels—motels—started to spring up on major routes. The first was the Milestone Mo-Tel, built in 1925 in San Luis Obispo, California.

Cars gave Americans a new

sense of freedom and independence. Most people had never been far from where they were born. Suddenly, travel became easier. People out in rural areas could go to town whenever they wanted. It opened up the country.

Besides the car, something else in the 1920s was changing how people spent their free time. Americans everywhere were going to the movies.

Milestone Mo-Tel

CHAPTER 7
Gilded Palaces

For about a quarter, people could sit in a movie theater and be taken to a whole new world, full of glamour and excitement. They could become lost in stories set in exotic settings, acted out on the screen by dashing men like Douglas Fairbanks and beautiful women like Lillian Gish or Gloria Swanson. They would laugh like crazy at the exploits of comedians such as Charlie Chaplin, Harold Lloyd, and Buster Keaton.

Before the main movie was shown, there might be live entertainment onstage featuring jugglers, singers, and even dog acts. Then one or two short films would be played, which might be comedies or cartoons. After that, there were newsreels, followed by trailers for upcoming films.

Clara Bow (1905–1965)

One of the biggest stars was Clara Bow. She represented the ultimate flapper: young, fun, sassy, and famous for her sultry eyes. The 1927 film *It* made her world famous and earned her the nickname the "It girl." That same year, she starred in *Wings*, the first film to win an Academy Award for Best Picture. Bow was able to make the leap to talkies (movies with sound) despite her Brooklyn accent, but after a number of scandals, Clara Bow retired from acting in 1933.

Finally, audiences would see the feature film, which could last up to two hours.

In cities and larger towns, even the theaters themselves seemed magical. A large, brightly lit marquee and ornate ticket offices near the sidewalk would lure in people. A sign might advertise that the theater was air-conditioned: a little slice of heaven on a hot, sticky summer day.

Builders created theaters that looked like opulent palaces and were decorated to rival elaborate European opera houses. A grand staircase would lead from the lobby up to the balconies. There were fancy carpets, fake marble statues, crystal chandeliers, and heavy velvet curtains draping the stage.

The style was often a mash-up of bygone times. Loew's 175th Street Theatre in New York City had an interior like a Hindu temple. Los Angeles had both Grauman's Chinese Theatre and his Egyptian Theatre.

Uniformed ushers would show customers to their plush, comfortable seats. Even the average person could feel as if they were being treated like royalty.

King Tut's Tomb

In 1922, British archaeologist Howard Carter discovered the tomb of a young ancient Egyptian pharaoh, Tutankhamun. It was the first time a pharaoh's tomb had been found with all its riches. There was gold everywhere, including the gold coffin that held the mummy of the boy-king. The discovery made news around the world. It also inspired Egyptian style in clothing, jewelry, and furniture in the 1920s.

Until 1927, movies had no sound. A piano or an organ might play music to accompany what was happening on the screen. In a large theater, there might even be a full orchestra to add to the experience. The Loew's Kings Theatre in Brooklyn, New York, had 3,676 seats. The Uptown Theatre in Chicago, Illinois, could hold 4,381 moviegoers.

Movie theaters were owned by the same companies—the studios—that made the movies. That way, studios such as Warner Bros., Paramount, and RKO had a guaranteed place to show the hundreds of movies that they made each year. Studios signed up actors and actresses for years. The studio head decided how stars would look, what they would wear, where they went, and whom they were seen with at nightclubs or fancy parties. Sometimes, the stars even had their names changed to something more glamorous. Gladys Louise Smith became Mary Pickford, who was known as "America's Sweetheart" because she played young, innocent girls. Lucille Fay LeSueur was transformed into Joan Crawford and was given roles of elegant and sophisticated women.

Joan Crawford and Mary Pickford

Rudolph Valentino (1895–1926)

Italian actor Rudolph Valentino was all the rage in the 1920s after appearing in the starring role in *The Sheik*. Women adored his dark, handsome looks and the romantic characters he played. When he died suddenly at the age of thirty-one due to blood poisoning and ulcers, his death caused mass hysteria. Female fans broke windows at the funeral home to try to view his body. Thousands lined the streets of Manhattan at his funeral.

In October 1927, the first movie with sound was released: *The Jazz Singer*, starring Al Jolson. (He performed with his face and neck painted black in some scenes. Even though "blackface" was a common practice at the time, it is now considered racist.)

Some of the songs and only ten seconds of dialogue had sound. Still, it was a breakthrough and a smash hit. Studios rushed to make more talking pictures, and theaters were quickly converted to sound. Unfortunately, not all the stars sounded as good as they looked, and some saw their careers fade away. But for those who had a pleasing voice, it opened up new possibilities. They could also perform on the radio.

CHAPTER 8
On the Air

It may seem like television has been around forever, but in fact it didn't become popular until the late 1940s. In the 1920s, instead of watching TV, people listened to the radio.

In 1920, the government granted KDKA in Pittsburgh, Pennsylvania, the first license to operate a public radio station. At first, the station was on the air for only an hour, but people tuned in.

Most had to build their own radios, which used batteries and were often unreliable. However, by 1925, the American Appliance Company was selling an electron tube that allowed radios to run on electricity. All people had to do was buy the tube and plug it in.

Radios became so popular that department stores added radio departments, and sales took off. By the end of the decade, more than ten million Americans had one in their homes.

In their living rooms, families gathered around the radio to hear news, music, live sports events, comedies, and dramas. Radios brought the news of the world into people's homes in a more immediate way than newspapers could. They created new

national heroes. In 1927, people listened to the thrilling story of pilot Charles Lindbergh and his heroic flight across the Atlantic Ocean.

Lindbergh had taken off from Long Island, New York, in his small plane, the *Spirit of St. Louis*. It had been stripped of as much weight as

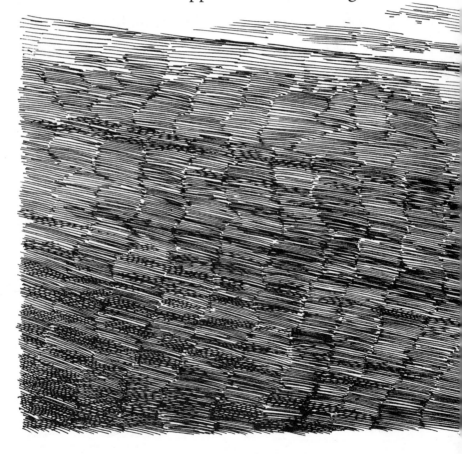

possible to carry a maximum amount of fuel. He had no copilot, no radio, not even a parachute. Flying was still quite risky, and others who had tried the crossing had been killed. Lindbergh—"Lucky Lindy" became his nickname—made it and landed at an airport near Paris 33½ hours later.

Air Travel

The first scheduled commercial airline flight in the United States was on January 1, 1914. The plane traveled twenty-three minutes between St. Petersburg, Florida, and Tampa, Florida. Its passenger was a former mayor of St. Petersburg, who paid $400 to sit on a wooden bench in the open cockpit. Early airplanes were built of lightweight materials, only able to carry light loads. In 1925, the Ford Motor Company built the all-metal Ford Tri-motor, which could carry twelve passengers. After Lucky Lindy's successful flight, interest in flying grew. By 1929, sixty-one passenger airlines and forty-seven airmail companies had been created, although at the time most airports were still only open fields.

Radio made national celebrities out of sports stars. Millions of people tuned in to follow college football and the exploits of Harold E. "Red" Grange, the "Galloping Ghost," who played football for the University of Illinois.

Broadcasters described in exciting detail the heavyweight championship fights between boxers Jack Dempsey and Gene Tunney, or gave thrilling play-by-plays of World Series baseball games.

And then there was the Babe. In the Roaring Twenties, George Herman "Babe" Ruth Jr. was a legend like no other. He was a powerful batter on the New York Yankees and the first sports

superstar. In 1921, he set a new season record of fifty-nine home runs. In 1927, as part of the Yankees lineup known as Murderer's Row, he hit sixty home runs, a record that lasted until 1961. Nicknamed "the Bambino," which in time was shortened to "Babe," he was a colorful character both on and off the field. He liked living large, spending lots of money on eating, drinking, and having a good time.

Sensational trials also captured public attention because of extensive news coverage. One of the most famous trials of the twentieth century was what the press called the Scopes Monkey Trial.

John T. Scopes

A young teacher in Tennessee named John T. Scopes had taught evolution in his science class. That may not sound like a crime. But in Tennessee it was, because Charles Darwin's theory of evolution went against the Bible's depiction of the world being created in six days.

Scopes was arrested. The most famous lawyer in the country, Clarence Darrow, offered to be his defense attorney. Darrow did a brilliant job. But the judge ruled that the only real question was whether Scopes had actually taught evolution. He

Clarence Darrow

had, and the jury found him guilty. He was fined $100, but the verdict was later knocked down and Scopes never had to pay. The trial was covered by more than a hundred reporters and broadcast on the radio by Chicago station WGN.

News and entertainment was now easily available everywhere. People living in parts of the country that once had been separated by distance and geography were now all listening to the same things. Radio in the 1920s was helping to create a national American culture.

CHAPTER 9
Spend, Spend, Spend

In the United States, there had long been the idea that having any debt—owing money—was a bad thing. People shouldn't buy what they couldn't afford. They should either save up the money for what they wanted or needed, or they should do without it.

In the 1920s, that way of thinking was considered old-fashioned. People liked the idea of having more than just what they needed. They wanted to have things that made their lives easier and more fun.

And there was plenty to buy: everything from toasters, popcorn makers, and electric coffeepots to ready-made clothes. Department stores and chains like J. C. Penney and Walgreens opened

stores across the country. Sears, which had once been a mail-order company, opened its first store, and by 1929 there were 319.

The idea of buying on credit spread beyond buying cars like Ford's Model T. People bought refrigerators, sewing machines, furniture, radios, and phonographs on installment plans. Often an installment plan included paying interest—a small extra monthly fee. With interest, the consumer

ended up paying more than the original price of the product. Still, it was a way for people to have what they wanted right away.

Another way to appeal to customers was through advertising. In the past, stores would put small ads in local newspapers to show what was for sale. Now advertising agencies created clever commercials on the radio and ran large ads in newspapers and magazines all over the country. The ads told people that if they wanted to look their best, be a success at work, or have a good life, they needed to buy a certain product. Ads used catchy phrases. Canada Dry was "the champagne of ginger ale." "Nothing like it" was the slogan for Tide detergent. "The flavor lasts" was used by Wrigley's gum. Campbell's proclaimed that it was "Real food in delicious soup."

Movie and sports stars were paid to be in ads. It made people think they were buying the same things used by their favorite celebrities. Babe Ruth did ads for Red Rock Cola. Clara Bow wore Maybelline mascara.

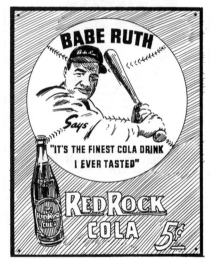

Companies needed to keep selling their product, over and over, often to the same customer, in order to stay in business. That presented a challenge to advertisers. Why would someone need a new car if the old one still worked? The answer was to make small changes to a product, maybe a different color or a slightly different design, and then use advertising to convince people that they needed this new, improved product that was much better than what they already had.

New body lines
DODGE BROTHERS
MOTOR CARS

Was all this shopping and spending a good idea? Some people didn't think so. Articles were written criticizing this focus on material things and the dependence on debt. But the economy was doing so well that no one could imagine a time when they wouldn't have money to pay off their debts. So people got out their wallets, and they bought and bought and then bought even more.

Burma-Shave Signs

Advertising could sometimes be very funny. Burma-Shave was a brand of brushless shaving cream that posted small signs along a road to attract the attention of passing motorists. Each sign had part of a silly rhyming poem and ended with the name of the product.

A poem from 1929 said:

CHAPTER 10
Not All Fun and Games

Times weren't good for everyone in the twenties. US farmers found it hard to make a living. During the war, prices for crops had been high. Many farmers had taken out loans to buy

more land and machinery to increase the amount of food they could grow. After the war was over, there was less need for all that food, and prices dropped. Many farmers couldn't pay back their loans and lost their farms. Between 1920 and 1932, one in four farmers lost their land.

Industries like cotton, wool, and coal suffered. The new women's fashions were made with a lot less fabric, and many textile workers lost their jobs, particularly in the rural South.

African Americans who stayed in the South rather than moving north struggled more than ever to make a living. Most were sharecroppers—farmers who didn't own any land. Instead they rented a small piece of property and farming supplies from a white owner. Sometimes sharecroppers had to give up to 70 percent of the crops they grew to pay back the debt. They were left with hardly anything.

Although people were moving out to the suburbs, many more were moving into cities. For the first time in US history, more people lived in cities than in the country. Farmers and people from rural parts of the country came looking for work. Immigrants came from other countries, looking for hope and a new life.

Many Americans distrusted the foreign newcomers. They competed for jobs with people who had been born in the United States. Most didn't speak English.

There was also a fear that immigrants held dangerous political views. In 1917, there had been a Communist revolution in Russia. It had overthrown the czar (ruler). Communists believed that everything belonged to the state; there could be no private businesses. The government would provide everything the people needed. This threatened American capitalism and consumer culture. When the Communist Party was established in the United States, many people became scared.

There was also a fear of anarchists, people who didn't believe in any type of government. Some people worried that anarchists would use violence to destroy the United States.

In 1919, anarchists exploded bombs outside the homes of several government officials in Washington, DC, including the United States attorney general, A. Mitchell Palmer. In 1920, another bomb exploded on Wall Street in New

York City. It killed thirty-eight people and injured hundreds. This led to government raids in which anyone who was even suspected of having anarchist or Communist ideas was rounded up. People were held without warrants, tossed into overcrowded and unheated jails on little evidence, or had confessions beaten out of them.

Sacco and Vanzetti

In 1920, Nicola Sacco and Bartolomeo Vanzetti, two Italian immigrants, were charged with robbery and murder. They were known to have ties with anarchists, but they denied they had committed the crimes. There was no real evidence against them. Still, they were convicted. The case drew worldwide attention. Protests were held on their behalf. People sent telegrams pleading for Sacco and Vanzetti to be pardoned or at least given a new trial. The appeals were denied, and the two men were executed in 1927. They were considered victims of the "Red Scare." (The Communist flag is red, and Communists were known as "Reds.")

Bartolomeo Vanzetti   Nicola Sacco

In 1924, Congress created the National Origins Act to reduce immigration. It put a yearly quota on immigrants.

Immigration from any one country was limited to 2 percent of the total number of people from that country who had been living in the United States in 1890. This meant that if only one thousand people from a country had been living in the United States in 1890, then only twenty people from that country could immigrate to the United States in 1924. This made coming to America impossible for millions of people. The act also banned any more Asian immigrants.

Those who managed to immigrate did not always have an easy time. They faced discrimination, which made it difficult to find work or places to live. Large families would be forced together in tiny, crowded apartments with little light and fresh air. Jobs were scarce. Often when they found work, such as in factories, the hours were long, the conditions unhealthy, and the pay very low.

Life for immigrants was always hard. But by the end of the decade, life was going to get hard for almost everyone in the country. And very few people saw it coming.

CHAPTER 11
The Good Times End

Before World War I, buying stock in a company was something done mostly by rich Americans.

Not anymore.

With the economy doing so well, ordinary people—those without much money—started buying stocks. They thought it was a way to get rich quick. (Buying a share or stock in a company means you own a small piece of that company.)

People thought the value of the stock of *any* company could only go up. And for a while, that seemed true. As more people bought a company's stock, its price rose, which caused even more people to buy.

Just as so many consumers were buying products on credit, people went wild buying stocks without having to pay the full price for them up front. It was called buying on margin.

So, say a person bought one share of a soda company. The price on the day it was purchased was $10. But the person only had to pay $2 right away for it. They'd have to pay the remaining $8 when they sold the share.

If the soda company's shares went up from $10 to $20, and the investor decided to sell his one share then, he'd still owe the $8. But he'd make a nice profit of $10. Sounds like a good deal, huh?

Even though shareholders didn't get any cash until they sold off their shares, in their minds they felt rich by simply owning the stock.

What they didn't consider was the risk . . .

Let's say the price of each share of the soda company stock dropped from $10 down to $5. If the investor had to sell it then, he'd only get $5, and he'd still owe $8. That means he lost $5 on the deal. So buying on margin could turn out very badly.

When people bought stock, the money went to the company who issued the stock. Companies discovered they could make a lot of money this way. They didn't need to take out bank loans anymore. This wasn't good for the banks. To make up for what they were losing, banks found other ways to get money. How exactly? They used their customers' savings to invest in the stock market.

Customers would also take out bank loans based on the value of stocks they owned. Maybe they wanted a loan to buy a new car or a new house, or even for buying more stock. They believed they'd be able to pay back the loan to the bank at any time, simply by selling their stock.

Soon everyone thought they were experts in investing. People would buy stocks based on rumors they'd heard. Comedian Groucho Marx said he got stock tips from an elevator operator.

Groucho Marx

Not everyone was convinced the economy would stay strong. Economists, people who study how money is made and used in a society, were concerned. They believed that many companies weren't worth nearly as much as their stock price made it seem.

A well-known economist, Roger Babson, was at a business conference on September 5, 1929.

He said, "Sooner or later a crash is coming, and it may be terrific." (By terrific, he meant awful.) He pointed out that factories were making fewer goods. Unemployment was rising, and wages were low for jobholders. With

Roger Babson

less money in their pockets, people were buying less . . . and the economy depended on people to keep buying more.

Stock prices reached an all-time high on September 3, 1929. Then they began to drop. On October 24, traders—professional people whose career was buying and selling stock—sold off a lot of overpriced shares. Seeing that, other investors sold their shares, which made even more people sell their shares. It was a classic snowball effect.

So many people sold shares that there was a huge drop in the stock market. On October 29, the market lost over $14 billion in one day. It became known as Black Tuesday. Panic set in.

Over the following days, people kept selling shares, and the market continued to fall. The stock certificates of many companies became worthless pieces of paper. Those companies folded, and their employees lost their jobs. Banks closed, having lost all of their customers' money. Nine million savings accounts were wiped out. People couldn't pay off all their debt and lost everything they had, including their homes.

The unemployed stand in line for free bread

It was the start of the Great Depression, one of the worst times in US history. The Roaring Twenties were over.

F. Scott Fitzgerald (1896–1940)

The great novelist F. Scott Fitzgerald wrote that during the 1920s, "America was going on the greatest, gaudiest spree in history." He also called it an "age of miracles, an age of art, an age of excess..."

Francis Scott Key Fitzgerald, named for a distant cousin who wrote "The Star-Spangled Banner," also popularized the term *Jazz Age*. He and his wife,

Zelda, seemed to be the dream couple of the Roaring Twenties—they were young, bright, and beautiful. And yet they both came to sad ends. Zelda died in a fire at a mental hospital where she was a patient. Scott was an alcoholic who died of a heart attack at forty-four.

Fitzgerald's most famous novel, published in 1925, is *The Great Gatsby.* It's a tragedy about a group of wealthy and privileged young people on Long Island, New York, in the summer of 1922. It is considered the book that defines the Roaring Twenties.

Timeline of the Roaring Twenties

1920 — Nineteenth Amendment gives women the right to vote

— Prohibition begins

— The Harlem Renaissance starts

1921 — Warren G. Harding becomes US president

1923 — Calvin Coolidge becomes US president after President Harding dies

— Cotton Club opens

1924 — J. Edgar Hoover is appointed head of the FBI

— Clarence Birdseye invents frozen foods

1925 — *The Great Gatsby* by F. Scott Fitzgerald is published

— John Scopes is arrested for teaching evolution

— American Appliance Company starts selling plug-in electric radios

1926 — Henry Ford announces forty-hour work week

— Rudolph Valentino dies

1927 — Charles Lindbergh flies across the Atlantic

— *The Jazz Singer* premieres

— Nicola Sacco and Bartolomeo Vanzetti are executed

1928 — Amelia Earhart is the first woman to fly across the Atlantic

— Herbert Hoover is elected US president

1929 — St. Valentine's Day Massacre takes place in Chicago

— Stock market crashes; Great Depression begins

Timeline of the World

1918 — Spanish flu pandemic begins

— World War I ends

1920 — The first Agatha Christie mystery, *The Mysterious Affair at Styles*, is published

1921 — Chanel No. 5 perfume is created by Coco Chanel

— Irish Free State is proclaimed

1922 — Gandhi preaches mass civil disobedience against British rule in India

— Mustafa Kemal Atatürk founds modern Turkey

— King Tutankhamun's tomb is opened by Howard Carter

1924 — Adolf Hitler is jailed after failed coup attempt

— The first Winter Olympics are held at Chamonix, France

— Vladimir Lenin dies

1925 — Benito Mussolini becomes dictator of Italy

1926 — Hirohito becomes emperor of Japan

— *Winnie-the-Pooh* by A. A. Milne is published

1928 — Alexander Fleming discovers penicillin

— The final volume of the *Oxford English Dictionary* is published

1929 — Edwin Powell Hubble proposes theory of expanding universe

— Richard E. Byrd and his crew are the first men to fly over the South Pole

Bibliography

*Books for young readers

Allen, Frederick Lewis. *Only Yesterday*. New York: Harper Perennial Modern Classics, 2010.

*KidCaps Presents: The Roaring Twenties: A History Just for Kids. Golgotha Press Inc., 2013. NOOK.

Lusted, Marcia Amidon. *The Roaring Twenties: Discover the Era of Prohibition, Flappers, and Jazz*. White River Junction, VT: Nomad Press, 2014. NOOK.

*Marcovitz, Hal. *Understanding American History: The Roaring Twenties*. San Diego, CA: ReferencePoint Press, Inc., 2013.

Margulies, Phillip, ed. *Turning Points in World History: The Roaring Twenties*. Farmington Hills, MI: Greenhaven Press, 2004.

Stillman, Edmund O. *The Roaring Twenties*. New Word City, LLC, 2015. NOOK.

Streissguth, Tom. *An Eyewitness History: The Roaring Twenties*. New York: Facts On File, Inc., 2001.

Websites

www.history.com/topics/roaring-twenties

Alvin "Shipwreck" Kelly perches on a flagpole.

1920s dance marathon competitors in Los Angeles, California.

Charles Lindbergh lands in Boston during a tour around the country, 1927.

Hollywood movie star Clara Bow

Flappers dance during a Charleston contest, 1926.

New York Daily News/Getty Images

Prohibition agents seize barrels of wine on the streets of New York City, 1921.

New York Daily News Archive/New York Daily News/Getty Images

Members of the Women's Christian Temperance Union crack open barrels of liquor after a raid, 1929.

A man kneels by directions to a speakeasy.

Louis Armstrong (center right, in dark suit) with a band in New Orleans,
Louisiana, 1920s

A crowd waits outside the Warners' Theatre in New York City
for the premiere of *The Jazz Singer*, 1927.

American actor Ethel Waters in the 1929 film *On with the Show*

Blues singer Bessie Smith, 1925

Henry Ford and his son sit in the fifteen millionth Ford Model T Car, 1927.

Assembly line workers inside a Ford Motor Company factory, 1928

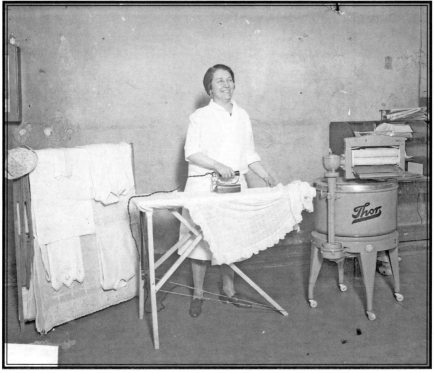

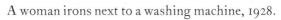

A woman irons next to a washing machine, 1928.

Actor Mary Pickford and her husband, actor Douglas Fairbanks

The Hollywoodland sign in Los Angeles, 1925

A stunt scene being shot for the silent film *Play Ball*, 1925

Artist Romare Bearden, who was inspired by the Harlem Renaissance, 1979

Flowers left by the star of Rudolph Valentino
on the Hollywood Walk of Fame